The Wolf

This book has been reviewed
for accuracy by

James Ward Rieder
Owner/Operator of Timber Wolf Farm's Foundation, Inc.
Greendale, Wisconsin

Copyright © 1991 Steck-Vaughn Company

Copyright © 1979, Raintree Publishers Limited Partnership

Library of Congress Number: 79-13309

5 6 7 8 9 10 11 12 13 14   99 98 97 96 95 94 93 92

Library of Congress Cataloging in Publication Data

Hogan, Paula Z
  The wolf.

  Cover title: The life cycle of the wolf.
  SUMMARY: Describes in simple terms the life cycle
of the wolf.
  1. Wolves — Juvenile literature. [1. Wolves]
I. Maxwell, Barbara, 1926- II. Title. III. Ti-
tle: The life cycle of the wolf.
QL737.C22.H63   599'.74442   79-13309
ISBN 0-8172-1507-7 lib. bdg.

The
WOLF

By Paula Z. Hogan
Illustrations by Barbara Maxwell

RSVP
RAINTREE
STECK-VAUGHN
PUBLISHERS
The Steck-Vaughn Company

Austin, Texas

 # The Wolf

The wolf's howl means many things. A pack howls together, warning strange wolves to stay away. One wolf may howl to tell the pack where it is.

The strongest male rules the wolf pack. Once he grows too old to keep order, another male fights his way to leadership.

The leader guides the hunt and
eats first. In large packs the leader's
mate rules the female wolves. She
is the strongest female.

Each wolf knows its place in the pack. The weakest wolf eats last. The others may attack it. When life becomes too hard, this wolf leaves the group.

12

If a lone wolf tries to join
another pack it may be killed.
Sometimes two lone wolves mate
and start a pack of their own.

13

The pack smells animals from
far off. When the leader picks up
the trail, the other wolves follow.

The pack hunts as a team.
Wolves circle an animal round and
round. When the animal starts to
run, the pack attacks.

18

Wolves hunt large animals. A healthy, full-grown moose is too strong for the pack to kill. They usually go after young or sick animals.

The leader and his mate have pups in spring. The whole pack helps feed and care for them.

All summer long the pups play and fight. The pup that fights best may some day be the leader.

The father wolf plays hunting
games with his pups. He chases
them over logs and through tall
grass. When he hides, the pups
try to track him down.

24

By winter the pups are strong
enough to run with the pack.
They may travel many miles
before finding food. Wolves can
go for two weeks without eating.

Wolves care for each other and obey their leader. Only by working as a team do wolves go on living.

coyote

jackal

fox

There are many animals that belong to the dog family. Like the wolf, coyotes, jackals, and foxes live in the wild.

GLOSSARY

These words are explained the way they are used in this book. Words of more than one syllable are in parentheses. The heavy type shows which syllable is stressed.

attack (at·**tack**) — to fight against

coyote (**coy**·ote *or* coy·**o**·te) — animal that looks like a small wolf and lives on flat, grassy land

fox — wild animal smaller than a wolf or coyote, with a long bushy tail and thick fur

full-grown — having grown up to become an adult

howl — to make a loud, long cry

jackal (**jack**·al) — a wild dog smaller than a wolf

leadership (**lead**·er·ship) — being able to rule over others

lone wolf — a wolf that lives and hunts alone

moose — a large animal in the deer family

pack — a group of wolves

pup — a baby wolf

strongest (**strong**·est) — the one who is most powerful

team — a group that acts together

weakest (**weak**·est) — the one who is least powerful